CONTENTS

9112/153047

MATERIALS

Recycling and reusing materials is good for the environment and it saves you pennies. With a little bit of know-how and imagination you can give used or unwanted items a new life. If you turn them into something even better, it's called upcycling.

socks

Socks

Who doesn't have a collection of odd socks? Give worn-out or lonely socks a new lease of life with an exciting craft project.

Stuffing

stuffing

You can reuse stuffing from an old pillow or cushion. If you don't have any, toy stuffing is also available in craft shops.

Buttons

Save the buttons from all your old clothes. If you need to buy extra buttons, look in craft shops or search online for really funky ones.

buttons

Printed paper

You can find loads of used paper in your home. Used wrapping paper, junk mail, envelopes and unwanted magazines are all perfect for paper projects.

Beads

You don't always need to buy beads. You can reuse beads from old, unwanted or broken jewellery. Just remember to ask an adult for permission before cutting anything up.

newspapers

envelopes

old jewellery

ties

ribbon
and braid

Ties

Ask your family and friends if they have any old or unwanted ties. If not, you can find cheap, second-hand ties in charity shops.

Greetings cards

Birthday and other greetings cards are far too pretty to throw out, so save them up and recycle them into something fabulous.

greetings cards

Ribbons and braids

You can collect ribbons from gifts and chocolate boxes. You can also buy ribbon and decorative braid from many craft shops.

Stretch elastic

Stretch elastic, also known as jewellery elastic, is available in craft shops. It is best to buy 0.6 mm or 0.8 mm thick elastic so you can thread tiny beads.

stretch
elastic

Brooch backs

To make sturdy brooches, you'll need to sew special brooch backs onto your material. You can buy these in craft shops.

brooch backs

5

TECHNIQUES
STARTING KNOT

When sewing, it is important to tie a knot in the end of your thread. This will secure the tail of the thread at the back of your fabric.

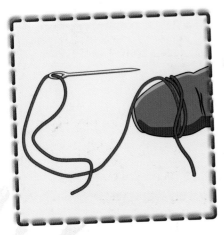

1 Wrap the thread around your index finger.

2 Using your thumb, roll the thread off your finger.

3 Pull the loop towards the end of the thread to make a neat knot.

THREADING

Use a single strand of thread for sewing thin fabrics. For thicker fabrics, or to make your stitches stronger, you can double the thread.

Single threading
Pass the thread through the needle and tie a knot in one end.

Double threading
Pass the thread through the needle. Make sure the needle is in the middle of the thread and knot both ends together.

Running stitch

Sew up and down through the fabric. Make sure the stitches on both the top and the underside are the same size and in a straight line.

Back stitch

Make a running stitch, then come up through the fabric a stitch ahead. Stitch backwards to meet your first running stitch. Repeat in a neat line.

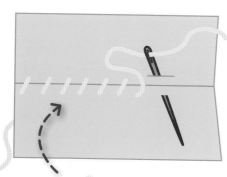

Whip stitch

Place the two edges of the fabric you are joining close together. Sew stitches from one piece of fabric to the other to bind them tightly.

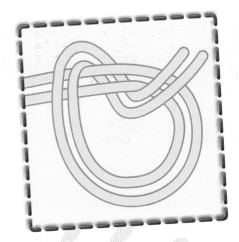

Elastic knot

Hold both pieces of elastic together and wrap them around your index finger. Pull through with your other hand. This is similar to tying a balloon.

Finishing knot

To finish sewing, make a small stitch and sew through the loop before pulling it tight. Repeat to make two knots. Cut off the excess thread, leaving a small tail.

BUTTON BRACELET

Make a beautiful bracelet out of buttons. Give it to someone special, or keep it for yourself!

YOU WILL NEED:

- 20-40 buttons
- Stretch elastic
- Paper clip
- Scissors
- Ruler

1 Collect 20-40 buttons (depending on their size and who the bracelet is for). Cut 25 cm of elastic (35 cm for an adult). Secure a paper clip 3 cm from one end of the elastic so the buttons won't fall off when you thread them on.

2 Thread the elastic through the front of each button, making the buttons overlap. If a button has two holes, thread the elastic through both. If it has four holes, thread it diagonally through two holes.

3 Wrap the bracelet around your wrist to check the size. A fairly snug fit is best as the buttons will stay flat. Remove the paper clip.

4 Tie the elastic using an elastic knot (see page 7). Cut off the excess elastic, leaving a 0.5 cm tail.

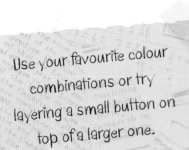

Use your favourite colour combinations or try layering a small button on top of a larger one.

ARMADILLO BROOCH

YOU WILL NEED:

- An old tie
- Paper
- Pencil
- Felt
- Two tiny buttons
- A brooch back
- Needle and thread
- Scissors

This quirky armadillo brooch is made from the end of an old tie. Make one to accessorize your clothes, or even a hat or bag.

1 Cut a 45 cm-long piece from the thinner end of a tie. Start rolling it up from the cut edge to make a cone shape. As you roll, use whip stitch (see page 7) to sew the fabric along one side. Roll the tie towards the sewing side.

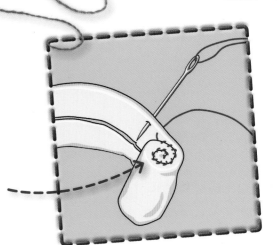

2 When you reach the pointy tip of the tie, fix it in place using a few stitches. You should now have a secure cone shape. This is the armadillo's head.

3 On a piece of paper, draw around the base of the head. Add two pointed ears. Using this as a template, cut out the shape from your felt. Sew the felt to the back of the head.

4 Open the brooch back and sew it onto the back of the head. Make sure that it is securely attached.

5 Sew the buttons on for eyes, going through the holes twice. Hide your finishing knot under the button.

Do you want a mouse as well? Make rounded ears and sew on a wool or ribbon tail.

11

CUPCAKE PINCUSHION

Have you finished with that bottle? Don't throw it away! Wash it out, find two odd socks and make a pincushion.

YOU WILL NEED:

- A used plastic bottle (rinsed clean)
- Two odd socks
- Stuffing
- A bead
- Ribbon or braid
- Needle and thread
- Ruler
- Scissors
- Craft or utility knife

1 Ask an adult to cut the bottom off a plastic bottle, about 5 cm from its base. A craft or utility knife is best for doing this.

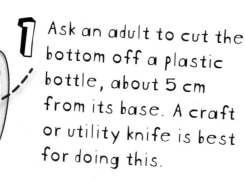

2 Measure 9 cm from the top of one sock and cut across. Discard the foot, leaving a tube of material. Pull the tube over the bottle so that the hem fits around the base. Tuck the cut end inside the bottle.

3 Fill the toe part of the second sock with stuffing, until it makes a firm ball. Tie the ball with double thread. Place the ball into the prepared bottle.

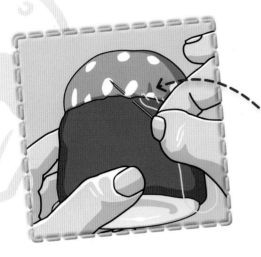

4 Using whip stitch (see page 7), sew the two socks together. Sew all the way around.

5 Sew ribbon or braid around the joined socks, using running stitch (see page 7). Top your pincushion with a bead. Now you have a perfect cupcake pincushion with a cherry on top!

You could decorate your pincushion with extra beads or embroidery stitches.

DRAGONFLY PEGS

These colourful dragonfly pegs are a great way to display pictures, photographs or important notes.

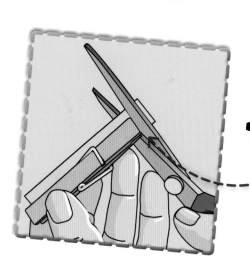

1 Spread glue on one side of the peg and stick a piece of paper onto it. Trim the paper so it is the same size as the peg.

2 On the plain side of your paper, draw a head, about the size of a ten pence piece. Cut two pieces of paper about 10 x 3 cm and 8 x 3 cm. Fold them in half and draw a wing on each one.

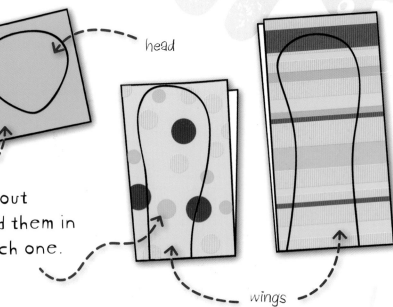

head

wings

3 Cut out the wings and head, and glue them onto the peg. Cut out a tail shape from the paper and glue it onto the end of the peg.

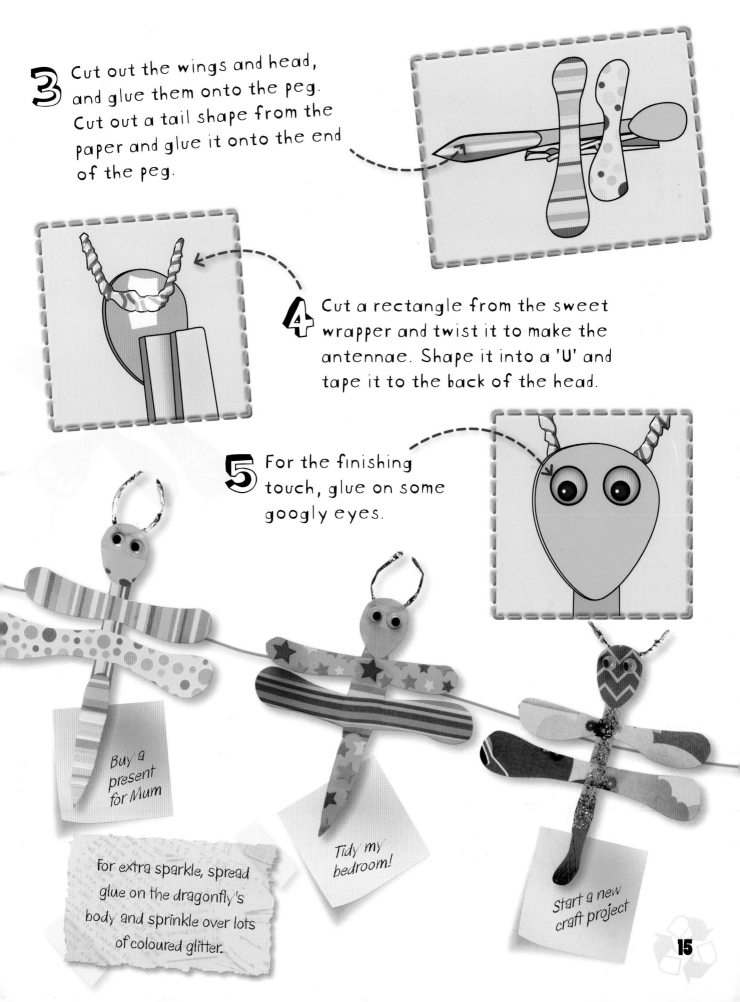

4 Cut a rectangle from the sweet wrapper and twist it to make the antennae. Shape it into a 'U' and tape it to the back of the head.

5 For the finishing touch, glue on some googly eyes.

Buy a present for Mum

Tidy my bedroom!

Start a new craft project

For extra sparkle, spread glue on the dragonfly's body and sprinkle over lots of coloured glitter.

GREETINGS CARD BOX

Recycle a used greetings card to make the perfect little gift box.

1 Cut the card in half. The front will be the top of the box and the back will be the bottom. On the inside of the card back, measure 3 mm from the top and the left. Cut these strips off.

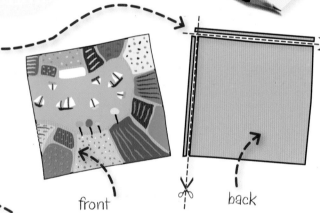

front

back

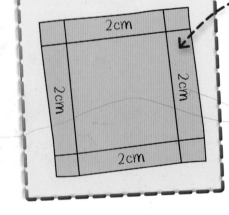

2cm

2cm

2cm

2cm

2 Now follow the same instructions for both pieces of card. On the insides, mark 2 cm margins all the way round.

3 Hold the ruler firmly on the margin and use the tip of the scissors to score carefully along the lines. Fold the margins up, using the ruler to keep the folds straight.

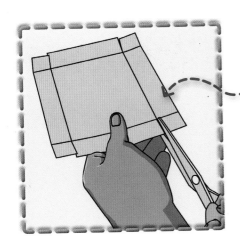

4 Cut two slits at each end of the cards to make four tabs per card.

tab

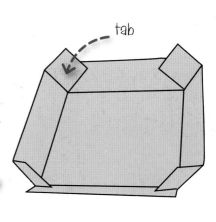

5 Put glue on the outside of the tabs and fold them in to make a box shape. Secure each corner with a paper clip until the glue is dry.

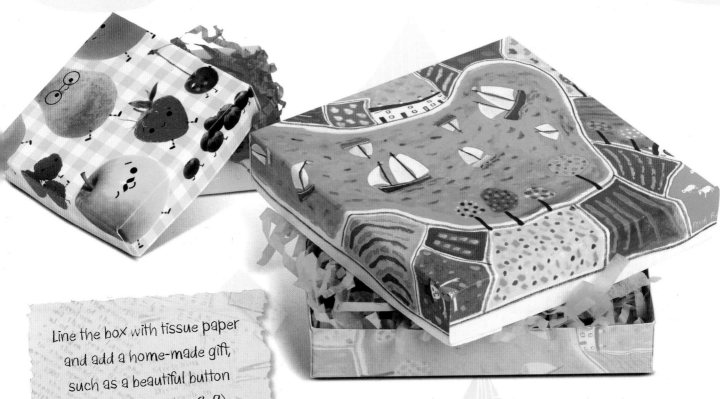

Line the box with tissue paper and add a home-made gift, such as a beautiful button bracelet (see pages 8–9).

JUNK MAIL JEWELLERY

Ask your friends to work out how you made your stylish jewellery. They'll never guess you made the beads from junk mail!

YOU WILL NEED:

- A 210 × 297 mm (A4) piece of junk mail or any used paper
- 8 cocktail sticks
- Glue stick
- Small block of polystyrene or block of modelling clay
- Small beads
- Stretch elastic
- Paper clip
- Clear nail polish or paper varnish
- Ruler
- Pen
- Scissors

1 On the back of the paper, mark 2 cm spaces down one side. On the opposite side, mark 1 cm from the top. Continue with 2 cm marks from this point. Using a ruler, join the marks to make about 20 thin triangles across the page.

1 cm

2 cm

2 cm

2 Cut along the lines you've drawn. You need 6-8 long triangles for one bracelet.

3 Starting from the widest end, roll a triangle snugly around the centre of a cocktail stick. Spread glue on the final **10–15 cm** of the paper and stick it down firmly. Do the same for each bead.

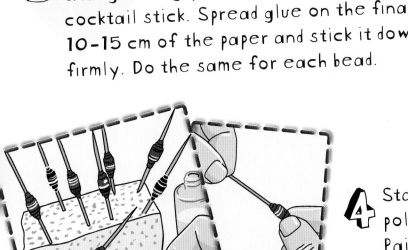

4 Stand the sticks in the polystyrene or clay. Paint each bead with a coat of varnish. Let it dry, then add a second coat. When they are dry, gently twist the beads off the sticks.

5 Cut a piece of elastic slightly bigger than your wrist. Attach a paper clip to one end. Thread on your junk mail beads, adding the smaller beads in between. Tie the bracelet with an elastic knot (see page 7).

How about making a bracelet from an old map?

PEG IT PRETTY

Upcycle some old cardboard and paper into a pretty picture display. Then find a good spot on your wall to hang your stylish creation!

YOU WILL NEED:

- Thick cardboard, e.g. an old box
- Ruler
- Glue stick
- 2 large sheets of different coloured paper, e.g. used wrapping paper or leftover wallpaper
- Strong double-sided sticky tape
- 5 flat buttons
- 5 flat wooden pegs
- Ribbon
- Scissors

1 Cut a 30 x 12 cm cardboard rectangle. Glue a slightly larger piece of paper to the cardboard. Tear six 20 cm-long strips of paper and glue them on. Fold and glue any excess paper to the back of the card.

2 Spread glue on one side of a peg and stick a piece of paper to it. Trim the paper so it is the same size as the peg. Do the same to all of the pegs.

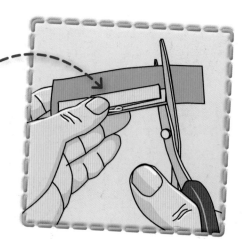

3 Place a piece of double-sided tape on the other side of each peg. Stick the pegs onto the cardboard, between the strips, with the squeezable part at the top.

4 Put double-sided tape on the back of each button. Trim off any excess tape and stick the buttons to the pegs.

5 Cut two loops of ribbon and stick them to the back of the cardboard, at the top. Cut a 28 x 10 cm piece of paper and glue it to the back of the cardboard, over the ribbons.

You could also use your pegs to hold jewellery or notes.

PLASTIC BOTTLE BLOOM

It's so sad when flowers droop and have to be thrown away. But this gorgeous bloom will last forever!

YOU WILL NEED:
- A mini plastic bottle about 10-12 cm high
- Pipe cleaner
- A large button
- A medium-sized button
- Chopstick or similar
- Very small cross-head screwdriver
- Small hammer
- Felt-tip pen
- Scissors

1 Remove any labels from the bottle. Ask an adult to use the hammer and screwdriver to bang a small hole in the lid of the bottle. Screw the lid back on the bottle.

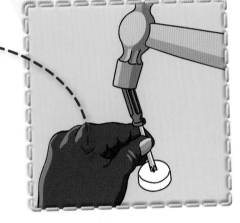

2 Using scissors, carefully cut the bottom off the bottle. Use a felt-tip pen to mark six dots equally spaced around the edge.

3 Use the dots to draw six petal shapes, from the bottom of the bottle to the edge of the lid. Cut out the petals and bend them backwards to open the flower.

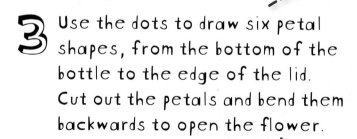

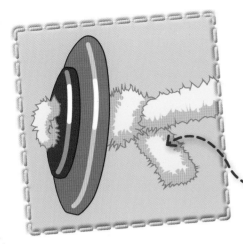

4 Thread the pipe cleaner through both buttons, with the smaller one on top. Make sure that one end of the pipe cleaner is twice as long as the other. Wind the shorter length around the longer end.

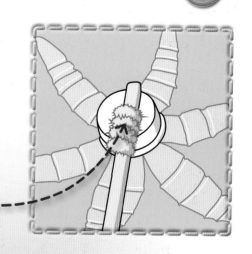

5 Thread the pipe cleaner through the hole in the lid. The button should cover the inside of the lid and the pipe cleaner will be at the back of the flower. Wind the pipe cleaner around a chopstick to make a stem.

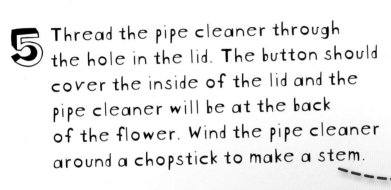

Make a daisy-like flower by cutting shorter petals with rounded ends.

SOCK MONSTER

Collect all your old or odd socks
and make a sock monster.

1 Turn the complete sock inside out. Lay it flat, with the heel on top. From the open end, cut through the middle of the sock, almost to the heel. These are the legs. Cut across the legs, about half-way up, to make two arms.

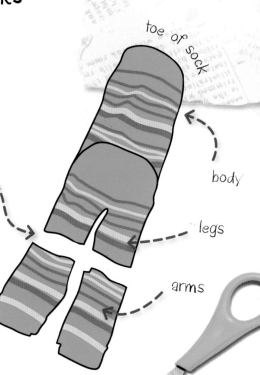

toe of sock

body

legs

arms

2 Sew up the end and side of each leg, using back stitch (see page 7). Leave a gap of about 3 cm between the legs for stuffing. Sew the arms using back stitch, leaving one short side open for stuffing.

3 Turn all the sock parts the right side out. Fill the sock with stuffing, including the legs and arms. Sew the gaps using whip stitch (see page 7). Sew the arms to the body with whip stitch.

4 Sew buttons on for the eyes. For the mouth, cut the stretchy cuff off the top of a sock and sew it onto the monster with whip stitch.

How about a hat? Just chop the toe off a sock to make your monster a beanie!

5 To make the hair, cut eight 1 cm-wide strips of varying lengths from your sock scraps. Sew them to the monster's head with running stitch (see page 7).

TOPSY-TURVY POT

Upcycle old paper into a stylish topsy-turvy pot! It looks cool and is great for storing all your crafty bits and bobs.

YOU WILL NEED:

- Used wrapping paper, junk mail or magazines
- Scissors
- Sticky tape
- PVA glue
- Paintbrush

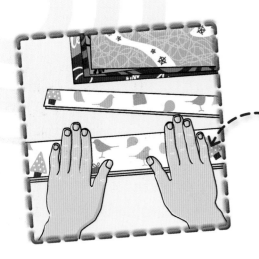

1 Cut twenty 15 x 30 cm pieces of paper. Fold each piece in half three times, lengthways. Secure both ends of each strip with a small piece of tape. You will have 20 strips which are about 2 x 30 cm long.

2 Wind a strip into a tight spiral and fix the end down with a piece of sticky tape.

3 Add a second strip to the spiral with some sticky tape. Wind it around the first spiral and stick the end down with tape. You will now have a bigger spiral. Continue adding strips until all 20 are attached.

4 Slowly and gently pull the circles up to make a bowl shape. The bowl can be straight or crooked, whichever you prefer. Be careful not to push too far, or your bowl may unwind!

5 Carefully paint the pot inside and out with PVA glue to help it hold its shape. Allow it to dry and then paint it twice more.

To add handles, glue or tape two small spirals on opposite sides of the pot and allow them to dry. Then add two mini spirals. Add three layers of PVA glue.

YO-YO BROOCH

Jazz up an old piece of clothing by turning it into a stylish yo-yo brooch.

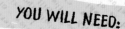

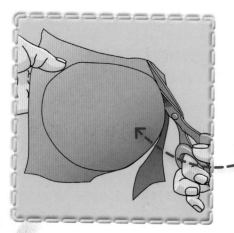

1 Use the bowl to trace a circle on the back of your fabric. Cut out the circle.

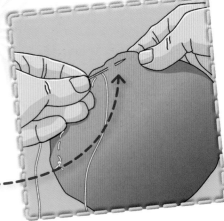

2 Cut 70 cm of thread and double thread the needle (see page 6). Sew running stitch (see page 7) around the front of the fabric, about 0.5 cm from the edge.

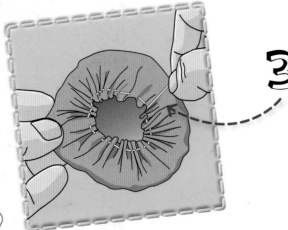

3 Without cutting the thread, gently pull it to gather the material together. Flatten the material. Make a stitch and knot where the pleats meet in the centre. Don't cut off the thread yet.

4 Using the same thread, sew the button over the pleat. Make sure that your stitches go right through to the back of the fabric.

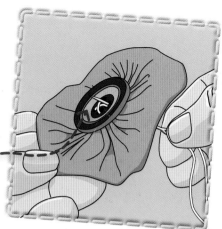

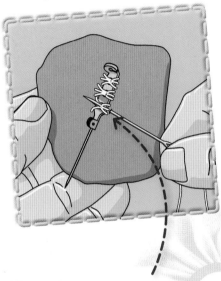

5 Sew the brooch back to the fabric, making 3-4 stitches through each hole to secure it.

For a layered brooch, make a smaller yo-yo brooch by drawing around a mug. Add a fabric circle between the two yo-yos and sew all three layers together.

EASY-PEASY GIFT BOW

Make your presents look fabulous by adding a home-made gift bow.

1 Cut the paper to 30 x 10 cm. Measure 1 cm from the narrowest edge of the paper and draw a line. Fold the paper along this line.

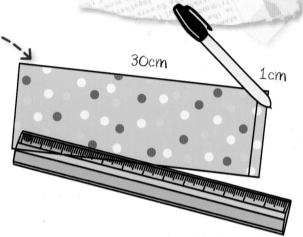

30cm

1cm

2 Fold the paper alternately forwards and backwards 1 cm to create a concertina. Cut both ends at an angle and fold the concertina in the middle.

3 Place the medium button on top of the large one and thread onto the string. Tie the string around the middle of the concertina, knotting it at the back.

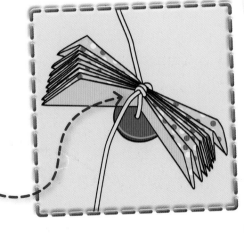

4 Spread glue along half of one side of the paper. Join the halves together, holding firmly to make them stick. Do the same with the other side to make a circle.

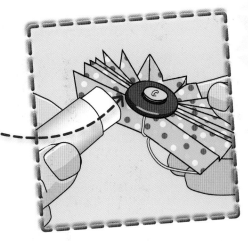

5 Add a strip of sticky tape to the back of the circle, where the paper joins. This will strengthen it. Tie your bow to a gift using the string.

Make the gift bow into a paper flower by tying the string to a chopstick, dowel rod or coffee stirrer.

INDEX